ANIMALS
in Art

Words that appear in **bold** type are defined in the glossary on pages 28 and 29.

Please visit our web site at: **www.garethstevens.com**
**For a free color catalog describing Gareth Stevens Publishing's
list of high-quality books and multimedia programs, call
1-800-542-2595 (USA) or 1-800-387-3178 (Canada).
Gareth Stevens Publishing's fax: (414) 332-3567.**

Library of Congress Cataloging-in-Publication Data

Baumbusch, Brigitte.
  Animals in art / by Brigitte Baumbusch.
    p. cm. — (What makes a masterpiece?)
  Includes index.
  ISBN 0-8368-4442-4 (lib. bdg.)
    1. Animals in art—Juvenile literature. I. Title.
  N7660.B33   2005
  704.9′432—dc22   2004057440

This edition first published in 2005 by
Gareth Stevens Publishing
A WRC Media Company
330 West Olive Street, Suite 100
Milwaukee, Wisconsin 53212 USA

Copyright © Andrea Dué s.r.l. 1999

This U.S. edition copyright © 2005 by Gareth Stevens, Inc.
Additional end matter copyright © 2005 by Gareth Stevens, Inc.

Translator: Erika Pauli

Gareth Stevens series editor: Dorothy L. Gibbs
Gareth Stevens art direction: Tammy West

Printed in the United States of America

1 2 3 4 5 6 7 8 9 09 08 07 06 05

ANIMALS in Art

by Brigitte Baumbusch

GARETH**STEVENS**

GS

PUBLISHING

A WRC Media Company

What makes an animal . . .

The whale shown above was carved out of black stone by Chumash Indians, who were Native Americans from California. The eye of the whale is a small shell.

Anasazi Indians made these little animals out of **pleated rushes**. The Anasazi people were **ancient** inhabitants of the Grand Canyon, in Arizona.

Prehistoric people from all over the world made paintings or **engravings** on rocks. Most of their rock art pictured animals. This group of storklike birds was engraved in ancient times on a rock in Tanzania, which is a country in Africa.

a masterpiece?

Animals have been art...

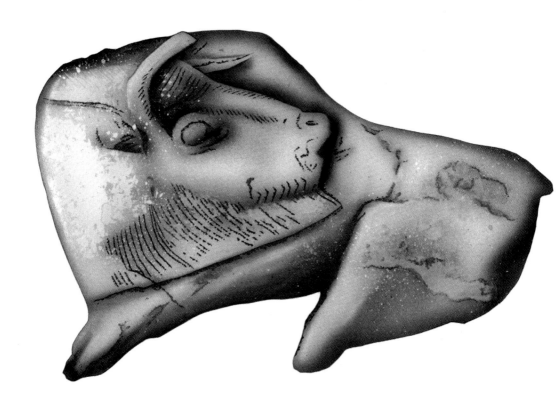

This bison, or buffalo, was carved from reindeer horn more than 17,000 years ago. At that time, humans still did not know how to **cultivate** fields to grow food. They mostly ate meat, which they got by hunting animals.

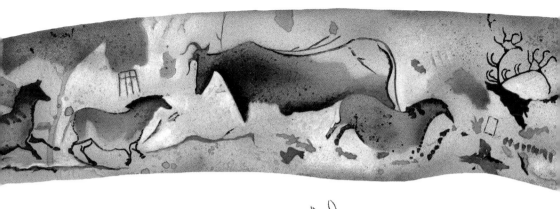

In the Stone Age, paintings with hundreds of pictures of animals sometimes covered the walls of entire caves. The animal paintings shown above were found in the caves of Lascaux, in France.

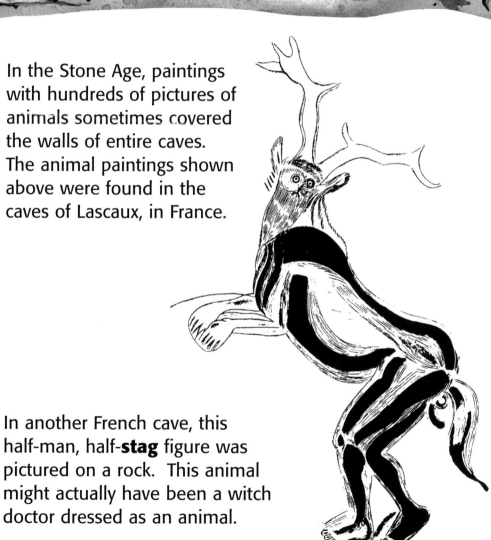

In another French cave, this half-man, half-**stag** figure was pictured on a rock. This animal might actually have been a witch doctor dressed as an animal.

from the very start.

Some animals are colorful.

Here, a Japanese **screen** shows a group of splendid roosters with multicolored feathers.

Others are . . .

This **woodcut** by M. C. Escher, a modern Dutch artist, is called "Sky and Water." Black birds in a white sky gradually turn into white fish in black water.

To make a woodcut, the artist carves out of a block of wood the parts of a design that are to remain white. Then the carved side of the block is coated with ink and pressed onto a sheet of white paper.

black-and-white.

Some animals are beauties.

A cat named Armellino had its **portrait** painted in the early nineteenth century. Behind the cat is a poem dedicated by the artist to the cat's **mistress**.

Albrecht Dürer, a German **Renaissance** artist, created this rhinoceros woodcut more than four hundred years ago. He had probably never even seen a rhinoceros — but had heard about them.

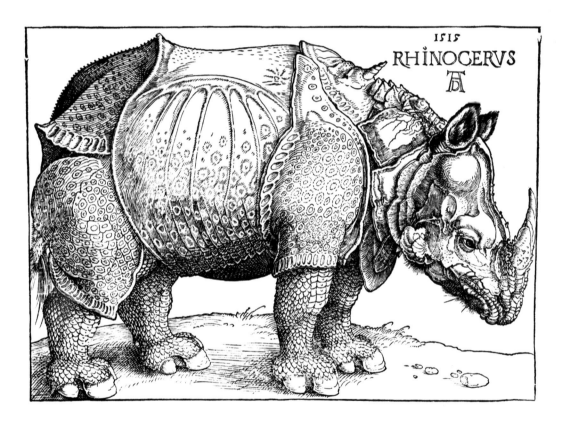

Some are beasts!

Animals move . . .

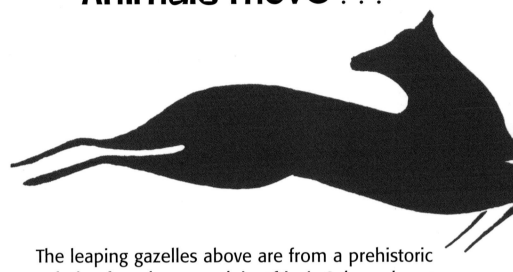

The leaping gazelles above are from a prehistoric painting found on a rock in Africa's Sahara desert.

The dog on a leash below is running as fast as its little legs can move. It was drawn in the early 1900s by Giacomo Balla, an Italian painter who enjoyed showing movement.

This ancient Chinese **figurine** made of **jade** (below) is a water buffalo resting with its keeper, who is just a child. In the Orient, water buffaloes are still used the way horses had been used in the Old West.

and lie still.

Animals can be gentle . . .

A flock of sheep walking in single file quietly heads for home after a day of grazing. This picture was painted at the end of the nineteenth century by an Italian artist with a complicated name — Giuseppe Pellizza da Volpedo.

Cats love to hunt. This cat with a bird in its mouth was painted by Spanish artist Pablo Picasso.

or vicious.

Baby animals
have mothers . . .

A lamb drinking its mother's milk is the subject of this four-hundred-year-old painting by Italian artist Jacopo Bassano.

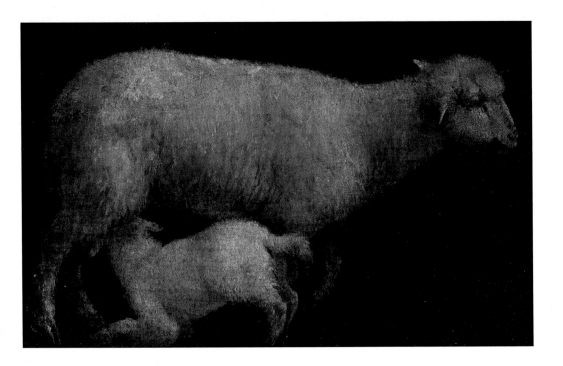

that take care
of them . . .

This beautiful example of **medieval sculpture** is a mother hen taking her seven chicks for a walk.

A mother rhinoceros plays with her calf in this prehistoric rock engraving found in the Sahara. Today, the Sahara is a desert, but thousands of years ago, the Sahara had rivers and lakes, as well as many plants and animals.

and play with them.

Many animals work for us.

This **terra-cotta** camel is a small decoration, but real camels are large animals that, for a long time and in many parts of the world, have been used to carry things for humans.

Horses are also **beasts of burden**. This little clay horse was made in Japan about 1,500 years ago. The **glazed** terra-cotta camel figurine (above) was made in China a few centuries later.

Twentieth-century French artist Henri Matisse created this painting, called "The Goldfish," in the early 1900s. While goldfish may not be very useful, they are pretty to look at.

Some animals make our homes prettier.

Pets are special animals . . .

Cats and dogs have always been most children's favorite pets. In the 1800s, this American girl had her portrait painted with her pets.

and special friends.

Snoopy, the famous beagle in the Charlie Brown cartoons, is Charlie Brown's pet dog and best friend.

When this tiny glass dog was made in Germany, more than two thousand years ago, it may have been just an ornament, or it may have been a child's favorite toy.

Animals can be magical . . .

The unicorn is a **mythical** animal that has never actually existed. As described by ancient Greek and Roman writers and depicted by artists of the Middle Ages, it looks like a deer or a horse with a long **spiraled** horn growing out of its forehead.

This famous French **tapestry** shows a captured unicorn inside a wooden fence.

bizarre . . .

Hieronymus Bosch, who lived in the
Netherlands five centuries ago, painted
many **bizarre** and unusual creatures.
This little man with a bird's head
is one of them.

or terrifying!

Like unicorns, dragons never
really existed, but they were
shown as terrifying **serpents**
or monstrous lizards — that
sometimes breathed fire!
The wild-eyed dragon
shown here was
painted on
a **porcelain**
Chinese vase.

Sometimes . . .

This lion, which is the symbol of Saint Mark the **evangelist**, is a painting on a page of a **Gospel** book that was written by hand in Ireland during the Middle Ages.

animals are symbols.

The ancient Egyptians often depicted their **gods** in animal form. This bird sculpture is an ibis. It represents Thoth, who was the Egyptian god of wisdom and magic.

The eagle has long been a symbol of power. For the Romans, it represented Rome's rule over the world. The eagle on this **medallion** was carved out of colored stone during the time of the Roman Empire.

25

Apes are the animals ...

In the picture below, monkeys are playing cards as if they were people. These monkeys were painted by David Teniers, an artist who lived in Flanders about three hundred years ago. Today, Flanders is known as Belgium.

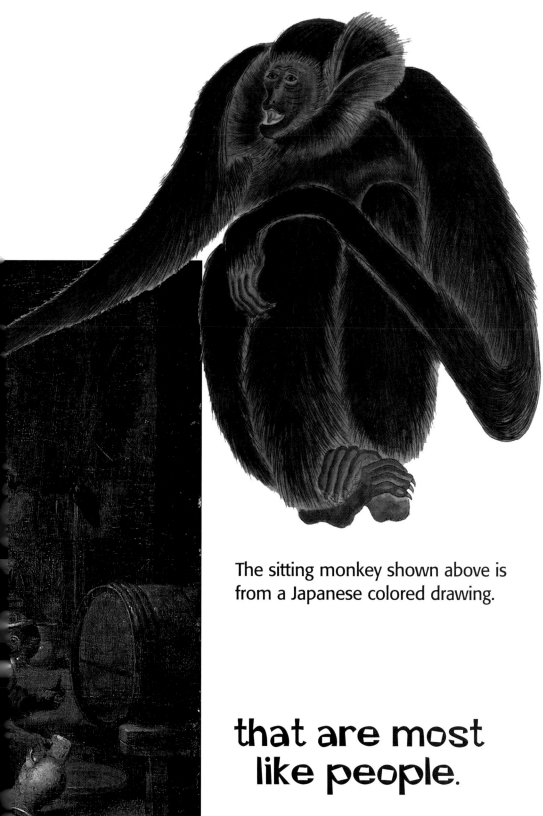

The sitting monkey shown above is from a Japanese colored drawing.

that are most like people.

GLOSSARY

ancient
relating to a period in history from the earliest civilizations until about the time of the Roman Empire

beasts of burden
large, strong animals, such as horses, oxen, camels, and elephants, that are commonly used to carry heavy loads, pull plows, and do other backbreaking work

bizarre
extremely unusual or unnatural in appearance or behavior

cultivate
to clear, loosen, and turn the soil in preparation for planting and growing crops

engravings
figures and designs cut deeply into hard surfaces such as wood, metal, or rock to form works of art

evangelist
one of the four Gospel writers in the Bible or a person who preaches the lessons of the Bible

figurine
a small, decorative, statuelike figure, usually made of china, pottery, wood, or metal

glazed
coated with a clear or colored paintlike liquid that dries to form a glossy and moisture-resistant surface

gods
spirits, beings, or objects believed to have supernatural wisdom and power

Gospel
the name given to any of the messages about Jesus Christ contained in the first four books of the Bible's New Testament

jade
a hard, green gemstone that is often cut and polished to make figurines

medallion
a large medal with a raised figure or design stamped into it, which is often given as a souvenir of an important event or a reward for some kind of achievement

medieval
belonging to the Middle Ages, a period of history in Europe from the end of the Roman Empire to the 1500s

mistress
a woman with authority or ownership over someone or something in particular

mythical
based on legends or traditional stories, called myths, rather than on facts or history

pleated
folded over and over onto itself in a continuous pattern

porcelain
a delicate white ceramic material used to make fine china dishes and figurines

portrait
a picture, photograph, or painting, usually of a person, that often shows just the person's head, neck, and shoulders

Renaissance
a period of European history, between the Middle Ages (14th century) and modern times (17th century), during which learning flourished and interest in classical (relating to ancient Greek and Roman civilizations) art and literature was renewed, or "reborn"

rushes
reedlike plants with long, usually tubelike, stems, which typically grow in marshy areas

screen
a flat, decorative panel used as a partition or to hide something from view

sculpture
a work of art created by carving, modeling, or molding materials such as wood, rock, stone, clay, or metal into a figure or object that is three-dimensional, instead of flat

serpents
snakes or snakelike creatures

spiraled
winding or coiled around and around in continuous circles, like a bedspring

stag
a male deer

tapestry
heavy fabric with figures or entire scenes woven, often by hand, into it

terra-cotta
brownish-orange earth, or clay, that hardens when it is baked and is often used to make pottery and roofing tiles

woodcut
a carving in a block of wood, which is coated with ink to make prints of figures, scenes, or designs

PICTURE LIST

page 4 – Whale in black stone with shell inserts. California Chumash Indians. New York, Judith Small Galleries. Drawing by Justine Thompson Bradley.

Animal figurines in pleated rushes. Arizona Anasazi Indians, c. 200 A.D. Santa Fe, School of American Research. Drawing by Lorenzo Cecchi.

page 5 – Drawing of storklike birds. Prehistoric rock art, c. 3000 B.C., Pahi (Tanzania). After a copy by Mary Leakey.

page 6 – Bison in reindeer horn. Magdalenian, c. 15,000 B.C., La Madeleine, Dordogne (France). Saint-Germain-en-Laye, Musée des Antiquités Nationales. Drawing by Lorenzo Cecchi.

page 7 – Detail of a painted frieze with animals. Magdalenian, c. 14,000 B.C. Lascaux Cave, Dordogne (France). Drawing by Lorenzo Cecchi.

Rock drawing of half-man, half-animal figure known as "The Sorcerer." Magdalenian, c. 12,000 B.C. Cave of Les Trois-Frères, Ariège (France). After a copy by Henri Breuil.

page 8 – Ito Jakuchu (1716-1800): Group of Roosters, panel of a screen. Tokyo, Museum of the Imperial Collections. Drawing Studio Stalio / Andrea Morandi.

page 9 – Maurits Cornelis Escher (1898-1972): Sky and Water I, 1938, woodcut. © 1999 Cordon Art B.V., Baarn, Netherlands.

page 10 – Unknown painter: Portrait of the Cat Armellino, early 19th century. Rome, Museo di Roma. Photo Scala Archives.

page 11 – Albrecht Dürer (1471-1528): The Rhinoceros, woodcut. Vienna, Graphische Sammlung Albertina. Museum photo.

pages 12-13 – Painting of running gazelles. Prehistoric rock art, c. 6000 B.C., Tassili N'Ajjer (Algeria). After a copy by Jolantha Tschudi.

page 12 – Giacomo Balla (1871-1958): Dynamism of a Dog on a Leash. Buffalo, Albright-Knox Art Gallery. Museum photo. © Giacomo Balla by SIAE, 1999.

page 13 – Jade figurine of a water buffalo and its keeper. Chinese art, Han dynasty, c. 100 B.C. Drawing by Justine Thompson Bradley.

pages 14-15 – Giuseppe Pellizza da Volpedo (1868-1907): The Mirror of Life. Turin, Gallery of Modern Art. Photo Fototeca R.C.S., Libri, Milan.

page 15 – Pablo Picasso (1881-1973): Cat Devouring a Bird. Private property. Photo Scala Archives. © Pablo Picasso by SIAE, 1999.

page 16 – Jacopo Bassano (1517-1592): Sheep and Lamb. Rome, Galleria Borghese. Photo Scala Archives.

page 17 – Hen with seven chicks in gilded silver. Medieval art of the 7th century. Monza, Cathedral Treasury. Drawing by Lorenzo Cecchi.

Engraving of rhinoceros and its young. Prehistoric rock art, c. 8000 B.C. Tassili N'Ajjer (Algeria). After a copy by Henri Lhote. Drawing by Roberto Simoni.

page 18 – Camel in glazed terra-cotta. Chinese art, T'ang dynasty, 8th to 9th century A.D. Drawing by Ivan Stalio.

Horse in terra-cotta. Japanese art of the 5th century A.D. Tokyo, National Museum. Drawing by Lorenzo Cecchi.

page 19 – Henri Matisse (1869-1954): The Goldfish, 1911. Moscow, Pushkin Museum. Photo Scala Archives. © Succession Henri Matisse by SIAE, 1999.

page 20 – Ammi Phillips (1788-1865): Girl in Red with Dog and Cat. New York, Museum of American Folk Art. Museum photo.

page 21 – Drawing of Snoopy from the comic strip "Peanuts" by Charles M. Schulz, reproduced with the kind permission of Peanuts © United Feature Syndicate, Inc.

Figurine of a dog in colored glass. Celtic art, 2nd century B.C., from Wallertheim, Palatinate Rhineland (Germany). Mainz, Mittelrheinisches Landesmuseum. Drawing by Lorenzo Cecchi.

page 22 – The Unicorn in Captivity. French tapestry, c. 1500. New York, Metropolitan Museum of Art, The Cloisters. Drawing Studio Stalio / Alessandro Cantucci.

page 23 – Hieronymus Bosch (1450-1516): Detail of the Temptation of Saint Anthony triptych (left wing). Lisbon, National Museum of Ancient Art. Drawing by Lorenzo Cecchi.

Dragon, from a Chinese porcelain vase, 15th century. Taipei, National Palace Museum. Drawing by Justine Thompson Bradley.

page 24 – Illuminated page from the Echternach Gospels. Medieval Irish art, 7th century. Paris, Bibliothèque Nationale. Drawing by Ivan Stalio.

page 25 – Bronze figurine of the god Thoth in the form of an ibis. Egyptian art, 5th century B.C. Turin, Egyptian Museum. Drawing by Lorenzo Cecchi.

Onyx cameo with the imperial eagle. Roman art, late 1st century B.C. to early 1st century A.D. Vienna, Kunsthistorisches Museum. Drawing Studio Stalio / Andrea Morandi.

pages 26-27 – David Teniers the Younger (1610-1690): Monkeys Playing Cards. Moscow, Pushkin Museum. Photo Scala Archives.

page 27 – Drawing of a seated monkey. Japanese art, Edo period, 18th to 19th centuries. Drawing Studio Stalio / Andrea Morandi.

INDEX

artists 9, 10, 11, 14, 15, 16, 19, 22, 26

Balla, Giacomo 12
Bassano, Jacopo 16
birds 5, 9, 15, 23, 25
Bosch, Hieronymus 23
buffaloes 6, 13

camels 18
carvings 4, 6, 25
cats 10, 15, 20
chickens (roosters) 8, 17

deer (stags) 7, 22
dogs 12, 20, 21
dragons 23
drawings 27
Dürer, Albrecht 11

engravings 5, 17
Escher, M. C. 9

figurines 13, 18
fish 9, 19

gazelles 12

horses 13, 18, 22

lions 24

Matisse, Henri 19
medallions 25
medieval art (Middle Ages) 17, 22, 24
monkeys (apes) 26, 27
movement 12

paintings 5, 7, 12, 14, 15, 17, 19, 23, 24, 26
pets 20, 21
Picasso, Pablo 15
portraits 10, 20
prehistoric art (Stone Age) 5, 7, 12, 17

rhinoceroses 11, 17

sculpture 17, 25
sheep (lambs) 14, 16
symbols 25

tapestries 22
Teniers, David 26
toys 21

unicorns 22, 23

Volpedo, Giuseppe Pellizza da 14

whales 4
woodcuts 9, 11